More!
Bible Crafts
on a
• Shoestring •
Budget

Chenille Wire and Plastic Straws

MW00380258

For information regarding the CPSIA on this printed material call:
203-595-3636 and provide reference # LANC-651218

rainbowpublishers®

An imprint of Rose Publishing, Inc.
Torrance, CA
www.Rose-Publishing.com

Chenille Wire and Plastic Straws

Donna Gentile

This book is dedicated to my loving husband, Nick, who has always been there to help and motivate me to become the best writer for God.

I would also like to say thanks to all my Sunday school children over the years who have helped to test the crafts in this book.

Lastly, I want to dedicate this book to my good friend Melbe, for without her encouraging words to teach, this book wouldn't be possible.

~ Donna Gentile

More! Bible Crafts on a Shoestring Budget: Chenille Wire and Plastic Straws
©2014 by Donna Gentile, eighth printing
ISBN 10: 1-58411-060-0
ISBN 13: 978-1-58411-060-6
Rainbow reorder# RB38015
RELIGION / Christian Ministry / Children

Rainbow Publishers
An imprint of Rose Publishing, Inc.
4733 Torrance Blvd., #259
Torrance, CA 90503
www.Rose-Publishing.com

Cover Illustrator: Paul Sharp
Interior Illustrator: Al Hering

SUSTAINABLE FORESTRY INITIATIVE Certified Sourcing www.sfiprogram.org SFI-00484

Printed in the United States of America

Table of Contents

Memory Verse Index

Introduction

Do your students enjoy making crafts? No doubt! Next question: Are you looking for crafts that are fun and inexpensive? *Bible Crafts on a Shoestring Budget* is your answer. Based on everyday items like chenille wire and plastic straws, these crafts are designed to get kids excited about the Lord. And with the reproducible patterns and easy instructions, you can save time to focus your energy on teaching the Bible.

Each chapter begins with a Bible story, which is matched with a memory verse and discussion starters. After each story, there are two craft projects that will help students retain the lesson's message and learn the memory verse.

This book is intended to make class time enjoyable for the teacher, too. Each craft page includes these sections:

What You Need: a materials list

Before Class: ideas for pre-craft preparation

What to Do: a step-by-step guide to completing the craft

(SAY) suggested talking points to help you relate the lesson

Adapt these lessons for your Sunday school or vacation Bible school class, your Christian day school art class or your own children at home. You will be reinforcing Scripture and stories from the Bible – the greatest book ever written – and creatively making a permanent impression on the heart of each child.

Obedience

Memory Verse

This is love for God: to obey his commands. ~ **1 John 5:3**

Abraham Is Tested

Based on Genesis 22:1-18

When Abraham was very old, God blessed him with a son named "Isaac." Abraham loved Isaac very much. God wanted to see if Abraham would love Him more than his own son, so He put Abraham to a test. If Abraham obeyed, God would know that Abraham was worthy of performing all of the wonderful things God had planned for him.

God spoke to Abraham: "Take your son Isaac and go to the region of Moriah. Sacrifice him there as a burnt offering on one of the mountains."

Abraham obeyed God. He saddled his donkey and started off with Isaac and two servants to the place where God told him to go.

Near the bottom of the mountain, they stopped. The servants waited there while Abraham and Isaac went up the mountain to worship God.

Isaac carried the wood while Abraham carried the knife and the fire for the wood. With a puzzled look upon his face, Isaac asked his father, "I see the fire and wood, but where is the lamb for the burnt offering?"

Abraham answered, "God Himself will provide the lamb for the burnt offering."

When they reached the area of worship, Abraham built an altar and laid wood on it. Then he tied up his son and laid him on the altar as a sacrifice.

Abraham obediently looked up to heaven and raised his knife to kill his son but suddenly an angel of the Lord appeared. The angel said, "Abraham! Abraham! Do not lay a hand on the boy."

Abraham hurriedly untied his son from the altar. They hugged, then they found a ram to sacrifice instead.

The angel said, "All nations on earth will be blessed because you have obeyed Me, declares the Lord."

Abraham went down on his knees to show his thankfulness to God.

For Discussion

1. If you were faced with a decision like Abraham's, what would you do?

2. Tell about a time when you had to do something difficult for God.

Blooming Joy

Instruct the children to place their vases of Blooming Joy on their kitchen tables as family reminders to obey God's commandments.

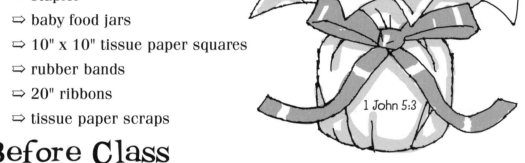

1 John 5:3

What You Need

⇨ flowers from page 13

⇨ scissors

⇨ chenille wire, three per child

⇨ stapler

⇨ baby food jars

⇨ 10" x 10" tissue paper squares

⇨ rubber bands

⇨ 20" ribbons

⇨ tissue paper scraps

Before Class

Duplicate the flowers from page 13 on yellow paper for each child. Make a sample craft to use as an example.

What to Do

1. Have the children cut out the flowers.
2. Instruct each child to coil an end of each chenille wire and twirl the other end (see diagram on page 13).
3. Each child should place a coiled portion in the center of each flower and staple it down.
4. To make the vases, have each child lay a baby food jar in the middle of a tissue paper square.
5. The children should wrap the tissue paper upward toward the necks of the jars and secure with a rubber band.
6. The children should write "1 John 5:3" on the bases of the jars, then tie the ribbons over the rubber bands into bows.
7. Show how to place the stems of the flowers inside the vases.
8. Allow the students to stuff tissue paper scraps around the stems to keep the flowers in place.

SAY

When you love God, you want to obey His commands. Like flowers that bloom with happiness when they have water and sunlight, we bloom spiritually with a beautiful joy when we choose to obey God's truth.

Worship only God.

Do not use God's name in vain.

Do not make idols.

Do not want what belongs to others.

Keep the Sabbath day holy.

Do not murder.

Honor your parents.

Do not tell lies.

Keep marriage promises.

Do not steal.

coil   twirl

Chenille Wires

Cheerful Giver Basket

This craft will help your children understand the obedience of tithing.

What You Need

⇨ lid cover and side band from page 15

⇨ scissors

⇨ hole punch

⇨ pencils

⇨ craft glue

⇨ small margarine tubs and lids

⇨ chenille wire

⇨ coins

Before Class

Duplicate the lid cover and side band from page 15 on colored paper for each child. Cut a slit and punch two holes in each margarine lid cover where indicated. Make a sample craft to use as an example.

What to Do

1. Have the children cut out the lid covers.

2. Instruct the children to print their names next to "From:" on the lid covers.

3. Have the children cut out the side bands and glue them around the tubs.

4. Show how to align a lid cover with a margarine lid and glue it down.

5. Have each child insert a chenille wire into the holes of a margarine lid as a handle and knot the ends underneath, then attach the lid to the tub.

6. Give each child a coin to put in his or her basket as a first tithe.

SAY

You have just put your first tithe into your Cheerful Giver Basket! All that we have comes from God. He wants us to show our faithfulness by becoming cheerful givers of the money we receive and bringing some to church to put it in the offering. God loves an obedient cheerful giver. If we obey God, He promises to bless us.

Cheerful Giver

From:

Genesis 22:1-18

Lid Cover

Side
Band

Tithes

God Blesses Me!

Cheerful Giver

I Obey God!

Forgiveness

Memory Verse

If you hold anything against anyone, forgive him, so that your Father in heaven may forgive you your sins.

~ Mark 11:25

Melting Heart

Based on Genesis 25:19-28; 27:1-45; 33:1-4

Isaac was married to Rebekah. They had twin sons, Esau and Jacob.

When Isaac was very old, he became blind. He knew he would die soon and that he needed to make his oldest son, Esau, the new head of the family. He told Esau to hunt for some animals so they could enjoy a special meal together. At that meal, Isaac would make Esau the new head of the family.

But Rebekah overheard Isaac. She wanted Jacob, her favorite son, to be made head of the family instead. So while Esau was out hunting, she told Jacob she would prepare the meal for Jacob to present to his father. That way, Jacob could pretend to be Esau and receive the blessing as head of the family before Esau returned.

Jacob took a tray of food to his father and said, "I am Esau, your first born." Jacob was so convincing that Isaac believed him and blessed him as the new head of the family.

When Esau returned, he prepared the special meal. Then he went to Isaac so they could enjoy their meal together. But Isaac was confused and wanted to know who he was!

Esau said, "Father, I am your son, your firstborn."

When Isaac realized Jacob had tricked him, he became angry and told Esau, "Your brother came deceitfully and took your blessing."

Esau was angry, too, because the blessing was very special to him. Esau vowed that he would kill Jacob for what Jacob had done. But when Rebekah heard Esau's plans, she warned Jacob to leave.

Several years passed. Esau still held a grudge against Jacob. One day, while Esau and his men were traveling, they ran into Jacob. But Jacob was a changed man – he was now a man of God. When Esau saw his brother Jacob bowing to him, he was touched. Esau's heart melted with love and forgiveness for Jacob. He ran over to hug his brother. They were filled with joy!

For Discussion

1. When you hurt someone, do you want to be forgiven? Why?

2. Why should you forgive someone who hurts you? Give several reasons.

Palm Tree of Forgiveness

This creative tree will help students to remember to forgive others instead of holding anger toward them.

What You Need

⇨ palm leaves from page 18

⇨ scissors

⇨ green plastic flexible straws, six per child

⇨ clear tape

⇨ 2" x 12" pieces of brown construction paper

⇨ brown clay

Before Class

Duplicate the palm leaves from page 18 on green construction paper for each child. Make a sample craft to use as an example.

What to Do

1. Have the children cut out the palm leaves.
2. Show how to join the straws together with the flexible portions near the tops and tape them together.
3. Give each child a sheet of brown construction paper. Each child should cut slits (fringe) on the 12" side of the brown construction paper, then cut it into four 3" pieces.
4. Show how to wrap each 3" piece, fringed side up, around the joined straws and secure them with tape, one underneath the next.
5. Demonstrate how to bend the flexible portions of the straws outward.
6. Instruct the children to tape each of their palm leaves onto separate straws.
7. Help the students insert the bottoms of their joined straws into mounds of brown clay.

SAY

Even though Esau did not get what he wanted – becoming head of his family – he received God's blessing by forgiving his brother, Jacob. If we follow God's plans for our lives, He will reward us, too, even if it is not always in the way we expect!

Suncatcher of Love

Help your students create this beautiful suncatcher as a reminder to love and forgive others.

What You Need

⇨ big heart and mini hearts from page 20
⇨ scissors
⇨ clear, self-stick plastic
⇨ pencils
⇨ plastic straws
⇨ dried flowers
⇨ colored straws, shredded
⇨ colored markers
⇨ hole punch
⇨ suction cups

FORGIVE

OTHERS

Mark 11:25

Before Class

Duplicate the big heart and mini hearts from page 20 on heavy paper for each child. Make a sample craft to use as an example.

What to Do

1. Have each child cut out a heart, then lay the heart against the plastic and cut around it, making a plastic heart.
2. Show how to open up a heart and lay both halves on a table, sticky sides up.
3. Help each child place a straw end at the bottom of one half of his or her heart, allowing the remainder of the straw to hang down.
4. Instruct the students to drop bits of dried flowers and shredded straws on the sticky sides.
5. Help the children place their second hearts, sticky side down, on top of the first, lining up all sides. Seal the contents, starting from the edges and working inward.
6. Allow the children to color the mini hearts, cut them out and punch holes where indicated.
7. Show how to slip the mini hearts onto the dangling straws and thread the hearts upward.
8. Instruct the students to punch holes at the tops of the clear hearts. Give each child a suction cup to hang a Suncatcher.

SAY

Hang your Suncatcher of Love in a sunny window at home. Whenever you find it difficult to forgive, glance at your Suncatcher and remember how much love God must have for you to forgive your sins. God wants you to follow His example and forgive others, too. Forgiveness is not easy, but God promises He will bless us if we obey.

Thankfulness

Memory Verse

Give thanks in all circumstances, for this is God's will for you in Christ Jesus. ~ **1 Thessalonians 5:18**

God Has a Plan
Based on Genesis 37; 39–42; 45

Joseph had eleven brothers who were very jealous of him because their father had given only Joseph a colorful coat as a gift. Joseph was his father's favorite, and that angered his brothers.

Then Joseph told his brothers about a dream in which he saw the sun, the moon and eleven stars bowing down to him. The brothers thought that meant that Joseph would rule over them, which angered them even more. They plotted to kill him. One of his brothers convinced the rest to sell him to travelers instead. They told their father that Joseph was killed by a wild animal.

Joseph was sold to Potiphar, one of Pharaoh's officers in Egypt. Joseph was put in charge of Potiphar's belongings. Potiphar's wife liked Joseph and wanted him for herself, but Joseph was loyal to Potiphar. This angered her. When her husband arrived home, she told him that Joseph tried to hurt her. Potiphar believed her lies, and Joseph was jailed.

When it was discovered that Joseph could interpret dreams, he was brought from jail to interpret Pharaoh's dreams. With God's help, Joseph told Pharaoh that the dreams meant there would be a lot of food for seven years but then there would be seven years with very little food. Because Joseph was so wise, Pharaoh put him in charge of storing the food for the coming famine.

When the famine arrived, Joseph's family was one of those that ran out of food. His brothers decided to travel to Egypt to purchase grain. They bowed before Joseph as they asked to make the purchase. Joseph recognized them right away, but they did not recognize him. Joseph remembered his dream of eleven stars bowing before him, and he realized his life had followed God's plan. He could save his family from starvation!

When Joseph told his brothers who he was, they were afraid of what he might do to them. They asked for forgiveness. Joseph said, "Do not be distressed and do not be angry with yourselves for selling me here, because it was to save lives that God sent me ahead of you." The brothers were thankful to God for the special plan God chose for Joseph's life.

For Discussion

1. What was God's plan for Joseph's life?

2. What kinds of plans do you think God has for your life?

Thank You, Lord!

The children will enjoy creating this thank You card to the Lord to say thanks for all He gives them.

What You Need

⇨ thank You card from page 23

⇨ hole punch

⇨ pencils

⇨ colored markers

⇨ chenille wires, three per child

⇨ beads, 15 per child

Before Class

Duplicate a thank You card from page 23 on heavy paper for each child. Punch holes where indicated on the front of the card. Make a sample craft to use as an example.

What to Do

1. Have each child fold the thank You card in half and open it up.
2. Help the children think of special thank You prayers to God.
3. Allow the children to write their prayers on the insides of their cards, followed by their names.
4. Instruct the students to close the cards, then color the items on the fronts of the cards.
5. Show how to curl a chenille wire around a finger.
6. Have the students insert the curled chenille wires in the holes on the fronts of their cards. They can secure them in place by bending down the ends.
7. Instruct the children to close the cards and add four or five beads to the end of each curly chenille wire.

SAY

[Say a thank You prayer to God.] We thank You, Lord, for never allowing us to go hungry, and for giving us warm homes. Most of all, we thank You, Lord, for giving us wonderful families to love. In Jesus' name, Amen.

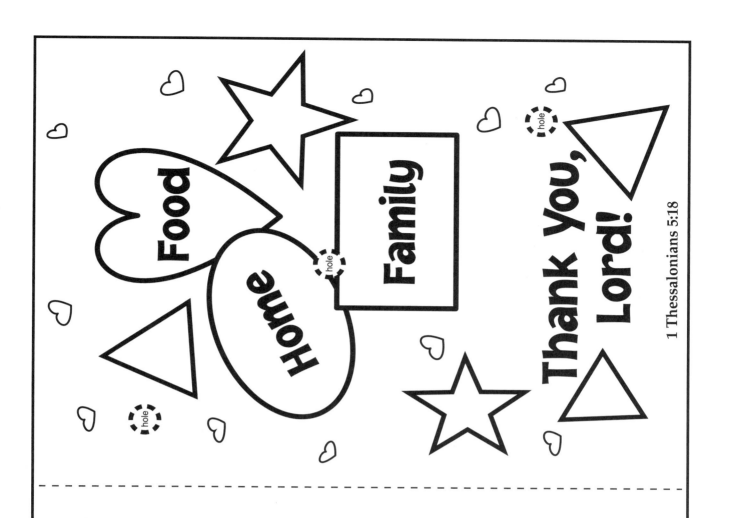

"Thanks for Loving Me, Dad!" Picture Frame

Have each child create a special gift for dad just to say thank you!

What You Need

- ⇨ frame and frame design from pages 25 and 26
- ⇨ cardboard
- ⇨ scissors
- ⇨ small pictures of students' dads
- ⇨ paper plates
- ⇨ craft glue
- ⇨ colored straw pieces, stripes and solids

Before Class

Duplicate the frame and frame design from pages 25 and 26 on heavy paper for each child. Lay each frame on a piece of cardboard and cut out both thicknesses, making one set for each child. Cut out the centers of the O's. Instruct the students to bring small pictures of them with their fathers or grandfathers (or closest father-figures). Make a sample craft to use as an example.

What to Do

1. Have the children lay the frame designs on paper plates.
2. Instruct the children to apply plenty of glue to the "L" and "V" letters. They should drop solid-colored straw pieces on the glue. Show how to shake off the excess and continue until completely covered. Discard the excess.
3. The students should do the same to the "O" and "E" letters, using striped straw pieces.
4. Allow plenty of time for the crafts to dry.
5. Help the children cut their pictures to fit and glue them behind the letter "O" on each frame.
6. Show how to bend the frames down, then have everyone print "1 Thessalonians 5:18" on the backs of their frames.
7. Have the students apply glue to the fronts of their frames, then show how to align the frame designs with the frames and join everything together.

SAY

Your relationships with your fathers are very special. God gave your dads a special gift: you! God wants all fathers to set good examples for their children and show how to obey God. So let's present Dad this gift to say thanks for all the love he shows you.

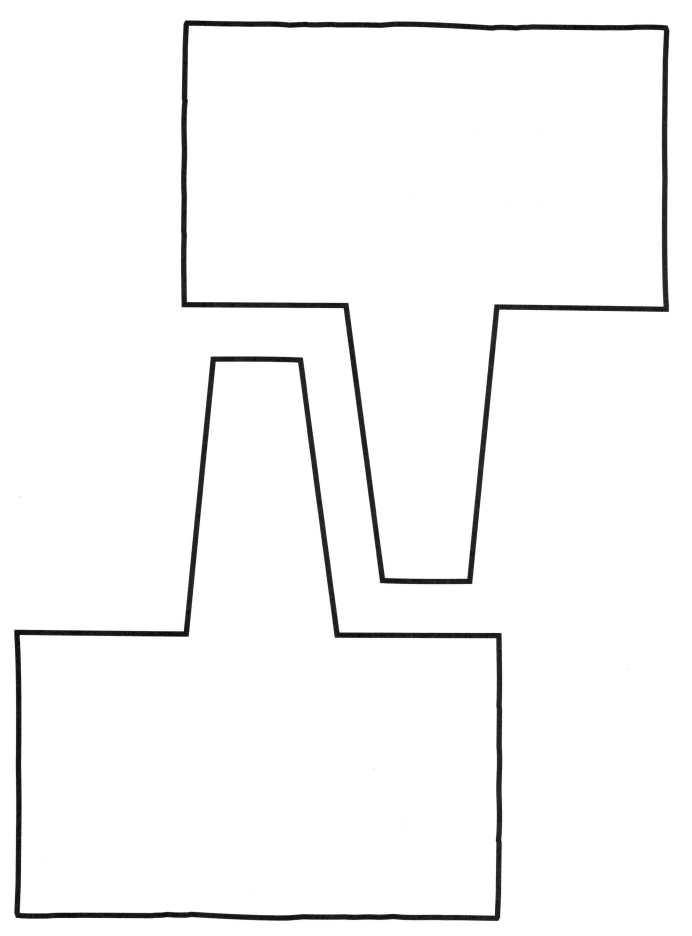

Dependence

Memory Verse

Be strong and take heart, all you who hope in the Lord. ~ **Psalm 31:24**

Hope in the Lord
Based on 1 Samuel 17:1-50

The Philistine army stood on one hill while the Israelite army stood on another hill, with only a valley in between. These enemies were about to fight one another when suddenly out of the crowd came an experienced Philistine warrior. The Israelites had to look up to see him! He was nine feet tall, wore heavy armor and carried many sharp weapons. He shouted down to the Israelites and their leader, Saul, to "choose a man and have him come down to me. If he is able to fight and kill me, we will become your subjects; but if I overcome him and kill him, you will become our subjects and serve us."

The Israelites were fearful. They lost all hope of winning the battle against the Philistines.

David, a shepherd boy, was walking to the battlefield to take food to his three brothers in Saul's army. When he got there, he heard Goliath's demands. David watched as the Israelite warriors ran away in fear.

David told Saul, "No one should lose hope because of this Philistine. I will go and fight him."

Saul replied, "But you are only a boy, and he is a warrior."

David convinced Saul that David could fight Goliath. David depended on the Lord for strength.

David left Saul and walked up to Goliath on the battlefield. David brought only his staff, five stones and a slingshot. At the sight of David, Goliath laughed loudly.

David said, "I come against you in the name of the Lord Almighty, the God of the armies of Israel, whom you have defied. This day the Lord will hand you over to me."

Then before Goliath could speak, David swung a stone from his sling and aimed it directly at Goliath. The stone struck Goliath in the forehead and he fell down dead.

It took a young boy to prove that when you depend on God, all things are possible. God can do wonderful things when we depend on Him to guide us.

For Discussion

1. Name some "impossible" situations you have faced.

2. Knowing that God makes all things possible, could you do what David did? Why or why not?

Take Heart!

Your students can give their heart cards to friends who need to know about depending on God.

What You Need

⇨ heart pattern from page 29
⇨ scissors
⇨ hot glue gun
⇨ fine-tip markers
⇨ craft glue
⇨ pillow stuffing
⇨ 7" x 8½" fabric pieces
⇨ 16" lace pieces
⇨ craft paint
⇨ chenille wire
⇨ plastic straws

Before Class

Duplicate the heart pattern from page 29 on heavy paper, making two for each child. Cut out all the heart patterns. Fold one heart in half and cut out the diamond on top. Cut apart another heart pattern to make two hearts. Make a sample craft to use as an example.

What to Do

Note: Do not let the children use the hot glue gun.

1. Have the children open up the folded hearts and print inside: "Because God poured His love into our hearts! (Romans 5:5) Love, Your Friend, [child's name]."
2. Show how to apply glue to one side of a single heart and apply stuffing to the glue, then trim off the excess.
3. Instruct each child to place the cloth fabric over the stuffing. Go around and use the hot glue gun to attach the fabric to the backs of the hearts.
4. Assist the children in gluing the lace to the back outer edges of the single hearts.
5. Show how to glue the single hearts to the fronts of the folded hearts.
6. Have each child print "hope" on a pillow heart with craft paint. Allow to dry.
7. Help each child secure a chenille wire through a plastic straw and tie the ends together. The straws may be placed inside the folds of the hearts for hangers.

SAY

Without hope, David would have run away from Goliath as the Israelites did. When difficult times come, we can have hope that God is with us. Do you have a friend who needs hope? Give your card to your friend. Tell your friend to depend on God, who is with us no matter what happens.

28

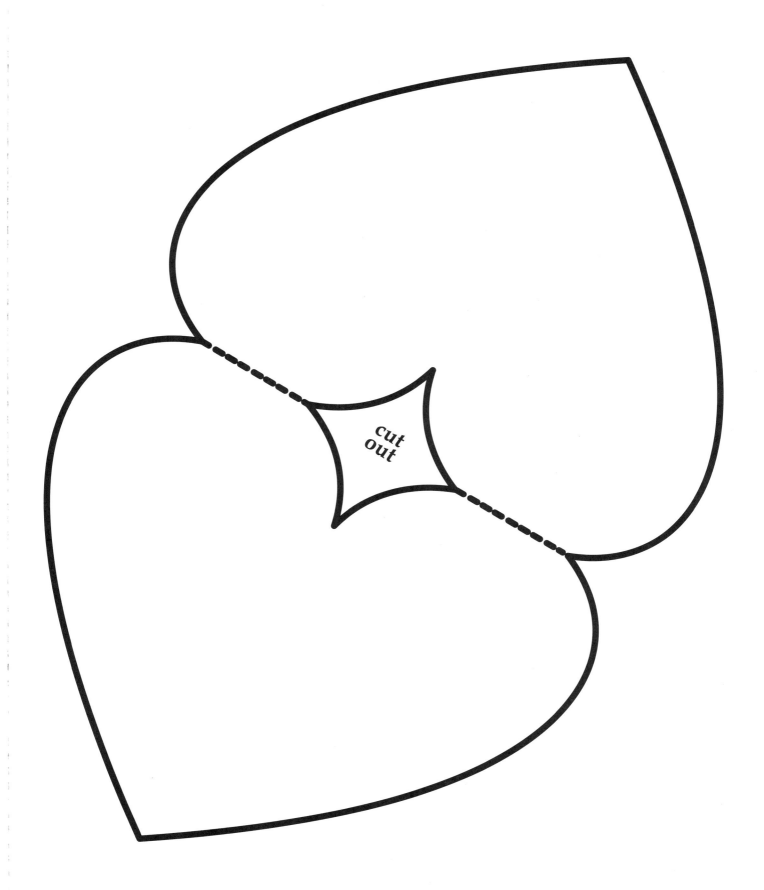

cut out

"Fear Not" Hat

The children can hang their Victorian hats on their refrigerators to remind them that they can depend on God for hope.

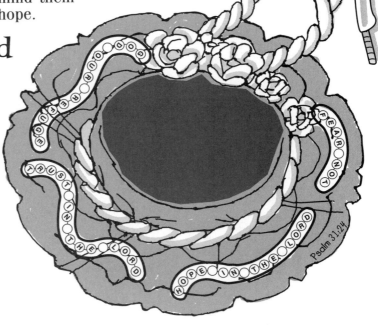

What You Need

- ⇨ string of pearls from page 31
- ⇨ 10" foil or paper doilies
- ⇨ small margarine tubs
- ⇨ rubber bands
- ⇨ burgundy chenille wire, two per child
- ⇨ white chenille wire, two per child
- ⇨ scissors
- ⇨ craft glue
- ⇨ artificial flowers
- ⇨ magnets

Before Class

Duplicate the string of pearls from page 31 for each child. Make a sample craft to use as an example.

What to Do

1. Have each child lay a doily over an upside-down margarine tub to form a hat. They should secure the doilies with rubber bands around the bases.
2. Show how to join two burgundy chenille wires into one. Do the same with the white wires.
3. Have the students join and twist together their burgundy and white chenille wires.
4. Show how to wrap the wires around the bases of the hats and tie each wire into a knot.
5. Have the children cut out the strings of pearls and glue them to the brims of their hats, then print "Psalm 31:24" on the brims.
6. Help the students cut off the rubber bands.
7. Show how to glue flowers near the chenille wire knots, and magnets to the backs of the hats for hanging.
8. After the hats are dry, remove the margarine tubs.

SAY

Hang your Victorian hat on your refrigerator to remind you of encouraging words of hope. Fear affects everyone. When you are feeling fear, think of the hope David had in knowing God was with him in all things.

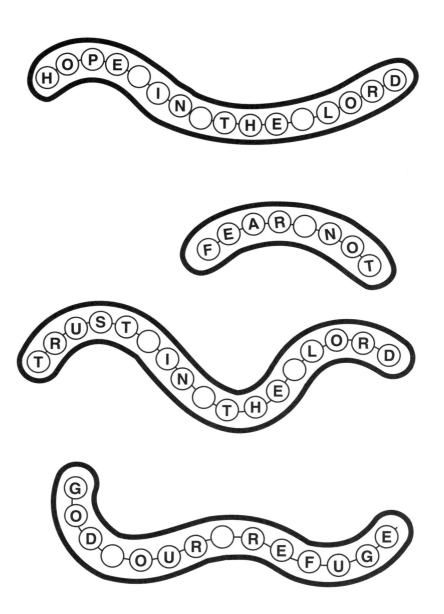

Best Friends

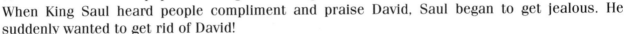

Memory Verse

A friend loves at all times.
~ Proverbs 17:17

A Special Friendship

Based on 1 Samuel 18–20

King Saul was impressed with a young boy named David who had killed the giant Goliath. So he invited David to join his household and live alongside Saul's son, Jonathan. From the moment David met Jonathan, they became best friends.

David did well at everything Saul asked him to do. He was also popular and good-looking. When King Saul heard people compliment and praise David, Saul began to get jealous. He suddenly wanted to get rid of David!

Saul gave the order to his officials to kill David. But Jonathan overheard and warned David to hide in the fields until Jonathan could convince his father to change his mind. Jonathan and David made an agreement to be best friends.

Later, Jonathan mentioned David's name to his father. King Saul became very angry. He thought Jonathan was taking sides.

Saul angrily said, "Go get him because he must die!"

"But what has he done?" Jonathan asked.

Saul became so angry he threw a spear at Jonathan, but missed. Jonathan knew now that his father truly intended to kill David.

The next day, Jonathan went to warn David to leave. David thanked Jonathan because without the warning, David would have been killed.

Before leaving, Jonathan and David hugged and cried. They knew they would miss their special friendship!

For Discussion

1. Do you have a special friend you would help no matter what the circumstances?

2. If your friend asks you to keep a secret, would you be able to keep it a secret? Why or why not?

Friends Love at All Times

A friend loves at all times.
Proverbs 17:17

Have the children create these gifts for their best friends.

What You Need

⇨ jar label and hearts from page 34

⇨ colored markers

⇨ scissors

⇨ baby food jars with lids

⇨ heart candy

⇨ craft glue

⇨ 5" diameter lace fabric circles

⇨ rubber bands

⇨ chenille wire, two per child

Before Class

Duplicate the jar label and hearts from page 34 for each child. Make a sample craft to use as an example. Bring extra heart candy for snacking.

What to Do

1. Have each child color and cut out a jar label and set of hearts.

2. Allow the children to fill their jars with heart candy. They should securely close the jar lids.

3. Show how to glue a jar label to the outside of a jar.

4. Allow the children to glue the hearts around the outsides of their jars as they desire.

5. Show how to lay the lace fabric over a jar lid and secure with a rubber band.

6. Demonstrate how to join two chenille wires into one and wrap them around the jar necks. Help the children tie the ends in small bows.

7. Give each child four heart candies to glue on the top of a lid.

SAY

Jonathan and David were best friends. They loved and trusted each other. Take time to give your best friends this gift to show them just how special they are and to let them know how thankful you are for them.

A friend loves at all times.

Proverbs 17:17

A friend loves at all times.

Proverbs 17:17

Big Bear Hug

The children will enjoy making Big Bear Hugs to give to their friends, along with real hugs!

What You Need

⇨ bear patterns from page 36

⇨ scissors

⇨ colored markers

⇨ craft glue

⇨ cotton balls, 14 per child

⇨ black chenille wire, two per child

⇨ white foam cups

Love bears all things.
1 Cor. 13:7 CEV

Before Class

Duplicate the bear patterns from page 36 on heavy paper for each child. Make a sample craft to use as an example.

What to Do

1. Have the children cut out their bear patterns.

2. To make the bear face, each child should color a face brown, leaving the eyebrows, eyes and nose white. Show how to glue half of a cotton ball on each ear. Have each child cut a black chenille wire in half, coil it flat and glue one on top of the cotton on each ear.

3. To make the bears' noses, have each child glue a cotton ball on the star in the middle of a bear's face, then glue the bear's nose on top of the cotton ball.

4. To make the paws, each child should glue six cotton balls to each bear paw. Each child should cut one black chenille wire into six equal pieces, then glue three (evenly-spaced) to the front of each paw.

5. Have each child color a heart.

6. Show how to turn the foam cups upside-down and glue the bear faces to the top backs of the cups, so the bear faces are facing you, then glue the bear paws around the middles of the cups and the hearts to the bottom fronts of the cups. Show how to dab the bear paws with brown markers.

SAY

Because Jonathan and David were best friends and loved each other, they chose to bear all things for the good of each other even if that meant not seeing each other anymore. Do you have a friend who is going through a difficult time? Give your friend a Big Bear Hug as a gift of encouragement just to let your friend know that you care. You may also want to give your friends real bear hugs so they know they are loved and can bear all things through Christ!

35

Love bears
all things.

1 Cor. 13:7 CEV

Right Choices

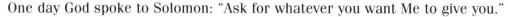

Memory Verse

Do what is right and good in the Lord's sight, so that it may go well with you. ~ **Deuteronomy 6:18**

Solomon's Wise Decision

Based on 1 Kings 3:3-28

Solomon became king after his father, King David, died. As a new king, Solomon wanted to do what was right according to God.

One day God spoke to Solomon: "Ask for whatever you want Me to give you."

King Solomon said, "I want a discerning heart so I can be a good leader who knows right from wrong."

Solomon could have asked for money or a long life. Instead, he thought of being a good leader above everything else. God was so impressed with Solomon's unselfish request that He made Solomon the wisest king of all.

Two women came to Solomon with a problem. Each woman had a young baby boy, but one night, one of the babies died. The mother of the dead baby switched hers with the other woman's living baby. When the other woman awoke the next morning, she found a dead baby. But when she looked closer at the baby, she realized he wasn't hers! She found her baby with the other woman. When she asked for her baby back, the other woman said it was hers instead. So they went to King Solomon so he could decide whose baby it was.

King Solomon listened to both sides of the story. Then he handed his official a sword and said, "Cut the living child in half. Give half to one and half to the other."

But the real mother said, "Give him to her! Don't kill him!"

The other lady said, "No, neither of us should have him. Cut him in two!"

Solomon then knew the baby belonged to the first mother. She was willing to give up her baby rather than have him killed. So Solomon returned the baby to the real mother.

The story of King Solomon's wise decision traveled throughout the land. The people knew he would be fair with them, too. They thanked God for giving their king wisdom to make the right choices.

For Discussion

1. If you pray and ask God for wisdom, will He give it to you?

2. Can reading the Bible give you wisdom to know the difference between right and wrong? If so, give an example.

Making Right Choices

These wise words will help your children make the right choices.

What You Need

- ⇨ flower, stem and leaves from page 39
- ⇨ Bible verse from page 40
- ⇨ carbon paper
- ⇨ pencil
- ⇨ foam sheets, pink & green
- ⇨ scissors
- ⇨ red markers
- ⇨ craft glue
- ⇨ large craft sticks
- ⇨ tinsel chenille wires, two per child
- ⇨ magnets

Before Class

Duplicate the flower, stem and leaves from page 39 on heavy paper. Using carbon paper, trace each duplicated item on an appropriate color of foam for each child. Duplicate the Bible verses from page 40 on heavy paper and cut out one for each child. Make a sample craft to use as an example.

What to Do

1. Have the children cut out each item from the foam sheets.
2. Have the children color the centers of the pink flowers red. Show how to glue the stems of the flowers to the craft sticks. Instruct the children to glue the pink flowers to the tops of the stems.
3. Show how to fold a chenille wire in half, bend it into a butterfly shape and twist it closed near the antennas.
4. Show how to attach an end of another chenille wire to the bottom of the butterfly.
5. Instruct the students to glue the other ends of their chenille wires to the bottoms of the stems, cutting off the excess. Show how to cover the chenille wire end on the stem by gluing green leaves over it.
6. Have each child glue a Bible verse to the middle of a stem.
7. Instruct the children to glue magnets to the backs of their flowers.

SAY

Keep this verse handy as a reminder of the wisdom King Solomon received from God. You, too, can make the right choices if you ask God for His help.

Do what is right and good in the Lord's sight, so that it may go well with you.
Deuteronomy 6:18

Do what is right and good in the Lord's sight, so that it may go well with you.
Deuteronomy 6:18

Do what is right and good in the Lord's sight, so that it may go well with you.
Deuteronomy 6:18

Do what is right and good in the Lord's sight, so that it may go well with you.
Deuteronomy 6:18

Do what is right and good in the Lord's sight, so that it may go well with you.
Deuteronomy 6:18

Do what is right and good in the Lord's sight, so that it may go well with you.
Deuteronomy 6:18

Do what is right and good in the Lord's sight, so that it may go well with you.
Deuteronomy 6:18

Do what is right and good in the Lord's sight, so that it may go well with you.
Deuteronomy 6:18

Bad Choices Have Roots

Encourage your students to hang up this craft so they can see how bad choices end in bad results.

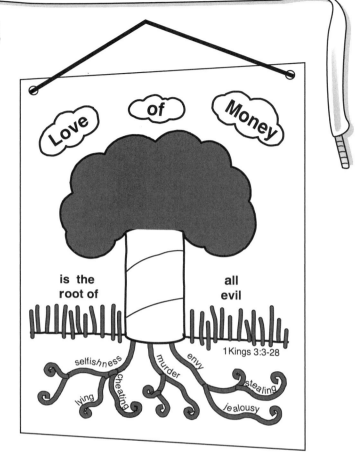

What You Need

⇨ tree picture from page 42
⇨ scissors
⇨ toilet paper tubes
⇨ brown crayons
⇨ blue and green markers
⇨ craft glue
⇨ ¼" green chenille strips
⇨ brown yarn
⇨ hole punch

Before Class

Duplicate the tree picture from page 42 on heavy paper for each child. Cut the toilet paper tubes in half lengthwise. Make a sample craft to use as an example.

What to Do

1. Have each child color a toilet paper tube half (to be the tree trunk) with a brown crayon.

2. The children should color the clouds blue in the pictures, and the top parts of the trees green.

3. Show how to place the toilet paper tubes where indicated and cut off the excess, then glue the tubes to the pictures.

4. Instruct the students to glue green chenille strips along the lines for grass.

5. Have the students cut brown yarn to make roots and glue it to their pictures.

6. Punch holes where indicated. Assist in tying yarn through the holes for hangers.

SAY

Hang your poster at home for your family to see. King Solomon could have asked God for anything, including money. But he knew that loving money too much can lead to bad things such as selfishness, lying, cheating, stealing, jealousy and even murder. Because King Solomon made the right choice and asked for wisdom instead of money, God not only gave him wisdom but also wealth and a long life. God blessed him, and He will bless you, too!

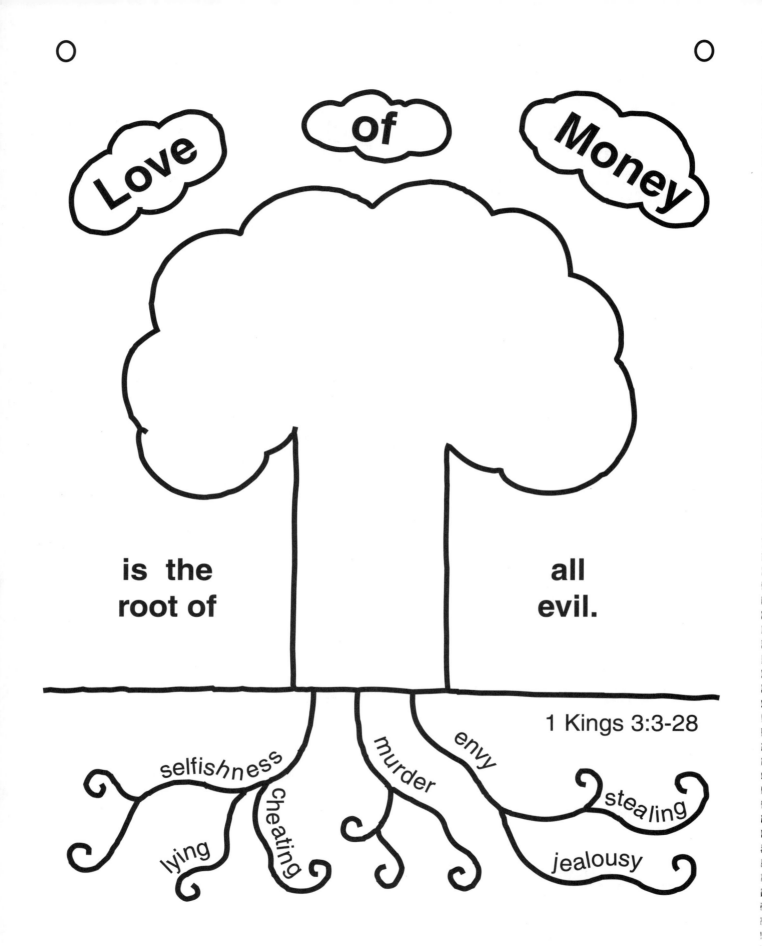

Love of Money

is the
root of

all
evil.

1 Kings 3:3-28

selfishness

murder

envy

stealing

lying

cheating

jealousy

Goodness

Memory Verse

Let your light shine before men, that they may see your good deeds and praise your Father in heaven.

~ Matthew 5:16

Wise Beyond His Years

Based on 2 Kings 22:1-13; 23:1-25

Josiah became king of Judah when he was only 8 years old! His father, Amos, was king before him. Amos was murdered for falling away from God and worshipping false gods.

Josiah was very different. He loved God and wanted to worship Him. So while he was growing up, Josiah studied all about God to gain wisdom.

When he became a young man, Josiah realized that many cities, including his own, were still worshipping false gods or idols. He wanted everyone to worship the real God. So he commanded that all idols be destroyed.

In the holy temple, King Josiah learned that there was an altar set up by past kings to worship false idols. He demanded that this altar be torn down and the temple be repaired so the people could have a place to worship God.

During the repairs, King Josiah's high priest found a scroll. After looking closely at it, he realized that it contained God's laws, the Ten Commandments, which Moses had received from God. God had given these laws to Moses to pass them from generation to generation. But somewhere along the way, the kings had forgotten those laws and began to worship idols instead.

The high priest took the sacred scroll to King Josiah to have it read to him. King Josiah realized that the people in his city were not following God's laws. He was so upset that he tore his clothes. Immediately, he called all the people to the holy temple and had the sacred scroll of laws read to them. The people were humbled and asked God for forgiveness. From that point on, their desire was to obey God's laws and do good for the Lord.

For Discussion

1. How was Josiah different from his father, Amos?

2. Which of God's Ten Commandments do you struggle with most in doing good for the Lord?

Good Mobile

Students will have fun creating this mobile with reminders of ways to do good for the Lord.

What You Need

⇨ church and church items from pages 45 and 46

⇨ scissors

⇨ chenille wires, two per child

⇨ craft glue

⇨ hole punch

⇨ 2" wood or plastic rings

⇨ colored markers

Before Class

Duplicate the church and church items from pages 45 and 46, making two sets for each child. Cut three 5-inch and one 7-inch length of chenille wire per child. Make a sample craft to use as an example.

What to Do

1. Have the children color and cut out the churches and church items.

2. Show how to glue the matching items together, back to back.

3. Instruct each child to punch one hole at the top of a church and three at the bottom. Everyone should also punch one hole at the top of each Bible, cross and choir.

4. Show how to attach one end of the 5" chenille wire through the hole at the top of the church, then attach the other end to a plastic ring (for hanging).

5. Have the students attach one end each of the 5", 7" and 5" chenille wires (in that order) to the three bottom holes of the church.

6. Show how to attach the other ends to the Bible, cross and choir (in that order).

SAY

Josiah's people learned God's laws from the scrolls. Where can you learn about God's laws? Church and Sunday school are two good places. Your pastor and church teachers can help you learn what God likes you to do. You, too, can do good for the Lord as Josiah and his people did. When you follow God's laws, you know you are doing good. Hang your Good Mobile in your room as a reminder to participate in church and Sunday school.

44

Let Your Light Shine

Your students can show off their lighthouses as their commitment to let their lights shine for Jesus by doing good deeds.

On the lighthouse illustration:

Let your light shine before men, that they may see your good deeds...

And praise your Father in heaven.

Matthew 5:16

What You Need

⇨ lighthouse from page 48

⇨ colored markers

⇨ scissors

⇨ plastic straws, two per child

⇨ tape

Before Class

Duplicate the lighthouse from page 48 on heavy paper for each child. Make a sample craft to use as an example.

What to Do

1. Have the children color and cut out the lighthouses.

2. Show how to insert one straw into the end of another straw to create one long straw (handle).

3. Have the students tape the top portions of the long straws to the backs of the lighthouses.

SAY

You can be like King Josiah, who was very wise even though he was young. The Bible helps you learn to be wise. Practicing what you learn shows others that you are trying to be good for the Lord. They will be able to see that radiant light coming from within you. Hold your lighthouse high to show everyone that you are a light who shines for Jesus!

Commitment

Memory Verse

No one can serve two masters. Either he will hate the one and love the other, or he will be devoted to the one and despise the other. ~ **Matthew 6:24**

Blazing Furnace

Based on Daniel 3:1-30

King Nebuchadnezzar was a very powerful king. He had a huge golden idol built, then commanded everyone to bow down to the idol when they heard certain music.

"Whoever does not fall down and worship will immediately be thrown into a blazing furnace," said the king. So when they heard the music, the people immediately bowed to King Nebuchadnezzar's golden idol.

Three Jews named Shadrach, Meshach and Abednego refused to bow down to the king's idol or any other false god. They loved and worshipped the true God.

When King Nebuchadnezzar heard about these three, he sent for them. When they arrived, they admitted that they were not bowing to the king's idol.

"If we are thrown into the blazing furnace, the God we serve is able to save us from it, and He will rescue us from your hand," the men said.

The king was so mad that he ordered his soldiers to tie up the men and throw them into the blazing furnace. He commanded that the furnace be heated seven times hotter than normal. It was so hot, in fact, that when the soldiers went to throw the three men into it, the soldiers were killed as the three men fell into the furnace.

After some time passed, King Nebuchadnezzar peered into the opening of the furnace. He yelled to his soldiers, "Look! I see four men walking around in the fire, unbound and unharmed." They all stood in awe because they knew the fourth person was God.

The king yelled into the furnace, "Shadrach, Meshach and Abednego, servants of the Most High God, come out!"

After the men left the furnace, the king noticed that there wasn't even a singe on their hair or clothes. With a humility he had never shown before, King Nebuchadnezzar said, "Praise be to the God of Shadrach, Meshach and Abednego."

Because of their commitment to God, the three men caused the king to believe in the real God. The entire kingdom was changed from idol-worshippers to God-followers!

For Discussion

1. What are some "idols" we bow to instead of God?

2. When others try to convince you to follow their "idols," how do you decide whether to go along or not?

49

Go On Green for God Necklace

The children can wear these necklaces as reminders that material possessions should not become idols.

What You Need

- traffic light and circles from page 51
- scissors
- egg cartons
- red, yellow and green markers
- craft glue
- hole punch
- chenille wires, two per child

Before Class

Duplicate the traffic light and circles on heavy paper from page 51 for each child. Cut out three egg sections as one group from an egg carton for each child. Make a sample craft to use as an example. Print "Matthew 6:24" inside the egg sections.

What to Do

1. Have the children color the traffic circles the appropriate colors.
2. Have them cut out the traffic lights and circles.
3. Show how to glue the hollow sides of the egg sections to the traffic lights.
4. Instruct the children to glue down the red, yellow and green circles (in that order), one in each of the egg sections.
5. Allow the children to punch two holes at the top of each egg section.
6. Show how to join two chenille wires into one, then insert them through the holes and tie them into a loop.
7. Have the children wear their creations as necklaces.

SAY

Money can become an idol. But, as a child of God, you can ask for His help to STOP on red and not think so much about money. Then you can proceed on yellow with CAUTION as the world tries to interest you in material things. When you put your commitment to God, you will be able to GO on green to be a light to the world as you learn to love "things" less and Him more.

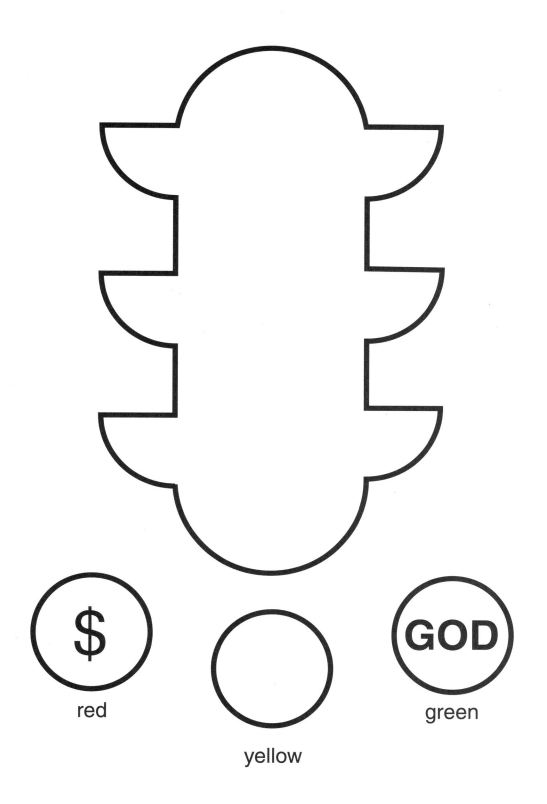

red

yellow

green

Blazing Furnace Door Hanger

The students can hang this message on their doors as cues to take a stand for God over the idols of the world.

What You Need

- ⇨ blazing furnace and characters from pages 53 and 54
- ⇨ scissors
- ⇨ red tinsel chenille wires
- ⇨ gray crayons
- ⇨ pencils
- ⇨ poster board
- ⇨ craft glue
- ⇨ colored markers

Before Class

Duplicate the door hanger and pictures from pages 53 and 54 for each child. Cut red tinsel chenille wires to various sizes to fit where fire is indicated on the door hanger. Make a sample craft to use as an example.

What to Do

1. Have the children color the door hangers gray above the flames.
2. Instruct the students to cut out the door hangers and the circles in the middles.
3. Have them trace the door hangers to poster board and cut them out.
4. Have the students glue the door hangers to the poster board shapes.
5. Instruct the children to color the other pictures and cut them out.
6. Have everyone glue the Shadrach, Meshach and Abednego picture on the left, above the flames, then glue "God" above the flames on the right.
7. Show how to glue the red chenille wire at the bottoms of the blazing furnaces where indicated.
8. Allow time to dry, then show how to bend back the tops of the chenille wires to give the hanger a 3-D effect.

SAY

Shadrach, Meshach and Abednego stood firm in their faith. God was with them because of their commitment to Him. God is there for you, too, when you need Him.

52

LOYAL to GOD

Daniel 3:1-30

Cut Out

Devotion

. . . .

Memory Verse

I call on you, O God, for you will answer me. ~ **Psalm 17:6**

Hear My Prayers, O God!

Based on Daniel 6:1-24

King Darius liked Daniel and chose him to keep watch over the kingdom. Some men were jealous of Daniel, so they looked for a way to make the king dislike him.

The jealous men knew Daniel was a faithful servant to his God. Three times a day, Daniel went home, knelt and devotedly prayed to God.

The jealous men went to King Darius and tricked him into signing a decree that would forbid anyone to pray to a god or man other than the king for 30 days. Anyone not obeying the decree would be thrown into a den of hungry lions as punishment. The jealous men knew, before the king signed the decree, that Daniel would continue praying to his God. They hoped Daniel would lose favor with the king and be punished. Then they would have a chance to receive the king's favor and keep watch over the kingdom.

After the king made the decree, the jealous men reported to the king that Daniel was still devotedly praying to his God. The king, who loved Daniel, was sad. He knew he had to punish Daniel because of the decree. The king could only hope that Daniel's God would protect him in the lions' den, just as Daniel believed.

The next morning, the anxious king yelled to Daniel in the den, "Daniel, has your God been able to rescue you from the lions?"

To the king's amazement, Daniel answered, "My God sent His angel, and he shut the mouths of the lions."

The king then knew that Daniel's God was the true God. Because of Daniel's devotion to prayer, the king came to believe in God, too.

For Discussion

1. How was God faithful to Daniel's devotion to Him?

2. When you pray, how can you trust that God will answer your prayers?

ACTS

Encourage the children to hang their ACTS close to their beds so they can follow these steps to be more devoted to prayer.

What You Need

⇨ ACTS sheet from page 57

⇨ scissors

⇨ chenille wire, four per child

⇨ ribbon

⇨ 10½" x 15" fabric

⇨ clothes hangers

⇨ craft glue

⇨ old buttons

⇨ craft paint

Before Class

Duplicate the ACTS sheet from page 57 on colored paper for each child. Cut chenille wire into two 7" lengths and two 8" lengths, one set for each child. Cut ribbon into two 9½" lengths and two 11½" lengths, one set per child. Make a sample craft to use as an example.

What to Do

1. Have each child fold 4" of fabric over the bottom of the clothes hanger and glue the flaps together.
2. Have the children glue the ACTS sheets down the middles of the fabric.
3. Show how to glue the 7" chenille wires over the top and bottom lines of the ACTS sheet and the 8" chenille wires over the left and right lines of the ACTS sheet.
4. Show how to glue down the 9½" ribbons over the top and bottom borders of the ACTS sheet and the 11½" ribbons over the left and right borders of the ACTS sheet.
5. Allow the students to glue buttons on their ACTS as desired.
6. Let the students cover over the lines inside the ACTS sheet with craft paint. Allow time to dry.

SAY

I encourage you to follow these steps to prayer, in order, when you pray: A stands for "Adore God" – speak praise to God; C stands for "Confess Sins"; T is for "Thank God"; and S is for "Submit Our Needs and the Needs of Others." Hang your ACTS near where you pray.

ACTS

Psalm 17:6

STEPS TO PRAYER

Adore God

Confess Sins

Thank God

Submit my needs **and the needs of others**

Recipe for Perfect Love

Have the children place Daniel's recipe on their refrigerators as reminders to not fear loving others.

What You Need

⇨ recipe for perfect love from page 59

⇨ scissors

⇨ colored straws, four per child

⇨ red markers

⇨ pencils

⇨ craft glue

⇨ magnets

Before Class

Duplicate the recipe for perfect love from page 59 on colored paper for each child. Cut straws into 5" lengths, two per child. You will also need two full-length straws per child. Using the tips of the scissors, cut open all of the straws. Make a craft to use as an example.

What to Do

1. Have each child cut out a recipe.

2. Instruct the children to color the hearts on the recipes red.

3. Have the children print their names after "From the Kitchen of:."

4. Instruct the students to glue magnets to the backs of their recipes.

5. Show how to apply glue inside the 5" straws and slide them onto the top and bottom borders of the recipes, then do the same with the full-length straws on the left and right borders of the recipes.

SAY

Daniel showed no fear in loving God by devotedly praying to Him, even though he knew he could be thrown into a den of hungry lions. We should all have this devoted love for God, and for others.

Recipe for Perfect Love

From the kitchen of:

_____

4 cups trust
2 cups loyalty
3 cups forgiveness
1 quart communication

3 T. hope
2 t. kindness
4 quarts honesty
no fear

Mix trust and loyalty well with honesty.
Blend with good communication and kindness.
Add forgiveness and hope, sprinkle abundantly
with no fear. Bake with sunshine and serve
generous helpings daily!

There is no fear in love.

1 John 4:18

Specialness

Memory Verse

I praise you because I am fearfully and wonderfully made. ~ **Psalm 139:14**

Arrival of a Special Baby

Based on Matthew 2:10-11; Luke 2:8-12, 21-38

For many years, people prophesied that a special baby was coming. This baby would become the Savior of the world! There were many people who noticed the signs of the baby's arrival.

As the shepherds were in the field watching over their sheep, an angel, one of God's messengers, appeared. He proclaimed to them the arrival of a special baby, Jesus.

At the very moment the wise men took notice of the brilliant star in the sky, they knew their wait for a Savior was over. This baby was special. They searched for Him and gave Him gifts. They knew He was the one who would save the world.

When Mary and Joseph brought baby Jesus to the temple, two other people saw Him and knew Him. God had chosen Simeon and Anna to be among the first of His people to see Jesus.

Simeon, a holy man, spent much of his time in the temple. He knew the Savior was arriving. God had revealed this to him through the Holy Spirit. Simeon learned that he would not die until he saw this special baby. Once Simeon took Jesus in his arms, he was in awe and knew this baby was that special One. Simeon praised God and said "My eyes have seen Your salvation, which You have prepared in the sight of all people."

Also in the temple, there was a holy woman named Anna. She spent all of her time praying, fasting and waiting for the arrival of the Savior. Once her eyes fixed on baby Jesus, she was in awe. She knew the Savior had finally arrived. Jesus was indeed a special baby.

For Discussion

1. Why were people so glad to see Jesus?

2. God makes each person special in his or her own way. What qualities make you special?

God's Messenger

Help the children make angels for their Christmas trees as reminders of who announced the arrival of the special baby, Jesus, the Savior of the world.

What You Need

- ⇨ backing and manger from page 62
- ⇨ colored markers
- ⇨ basket-style coffee filters, three per child
- ⇨ scissors
- ⇨ chenille wire
- ⇨ craft glue
- ⇨ 10" ribbon
- ⇨ cotton balls
- ⇨ 24" ribbon
- ⇨ 3" chenille wires
- ⇨ 4" chenille wires, two per child

Before Class

Duplicate the backing and manger from page 62 on heavy paper for each child. Make a sample craft to use as an example.

What to Do

1. Have the children color the sections as indicated on the backing patterns, then cut out the backings and lay them flat on a table.
2. Show how to fold the first coffee filter in half, then fold the chenille wires in half and glue the ends to the back of the filter.
3. With the fold of the filter on top, show how to glue it down on the straight edge of the backing (first note where the second and third filters will be glued).
4. Have the students glue the 10" ribbons on the folds of their filters first.
5. Show how to grab the center of the second filter and run your other hand downward on the filter to compress it. Have each student glue the second filter where indicated on the backing.
6. Instruct each student to grab the center of the third filter and compress it, then glue the third filter where indicated on the backing. Show how to glue a cotton ball (angel's head) at the top of the third filter.
7. Instruct the children to join the ends of their 3" chenille wires together and twist them closed, then glue them to their angels' heads for halos.
8. Help the students form 24" ribbons into bows and glue one under each angel's head.
9. Have the students coil their 4" chenille wire flat and glue them down on each side of their angels' wings. Allow the children to color the mangers, cut them out and glue them near the angels' feet.

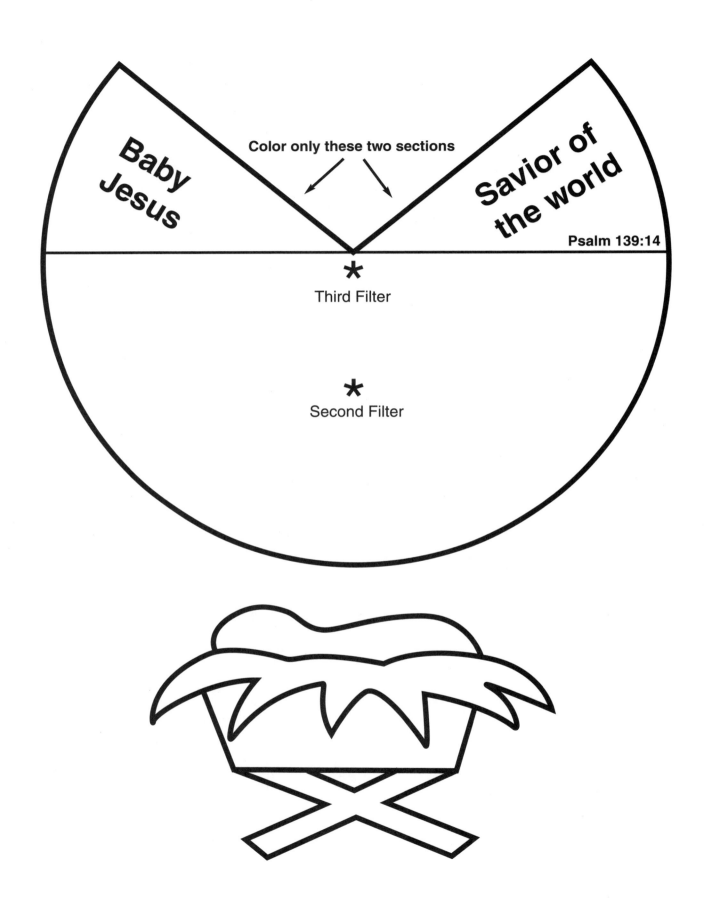

Baby Jesus

Color only these two sections

Savior of the world

Psalm 139:14

* Third Filter

* Second Filter

You're Special Wreath

Creating this wreath will remind your students how special they are.

What You Need

- clouds from page 64
- artificial flowers
- blue markers
- scissors
- 12-oz. foam bowls
- hole punch
- chenille wires, two per child
- craft glue
- dried brown moss

Before Class

Duplicate the clouds from page 64 on heavy paper for each child. Separate the petals and leaves from the flowers. Make a sample craft to use as an example.

What to Do

1. Have the children color the clouds blue and cut them out.
2. Each child should cut a rim off of a foam bowl for a wreath. Show where to punch two holes along the rim of each wreath for a hanger.
3. Show how to insert a chenille wire through the holes on the rim and connect the ends together.
4. Instruct the students to lay their wreaths on a flat surface and cover the rims with craft glue. Allow the children to apply small amounts of dried brown moss to the rims and press it down.
5. They should glue down the "Give Thanks to God" clouds to the rims below the chenille wire hangers.
6. Underneath, the children should glue the "You're" and "Special" clouds to the left and right sides.
7. Have the students glue the petals and leaves near the bottoms of their wreaths.

SAY

You were fearfully and wonderfully made by God! You can have fun learning what makes your friends special, too. You may even want to meet new friends just to see what gifts God has given them to make them special and different from you.

Self-Control

Memory Verse

When you are tempted, [God] will also provide a way out so that you can stand up under it. ~ **1 Corinthians 10:13**

Resist Temptation with God's Word

Based on Matthew 4:1-11

After John baptized Jesus, the Holy Spirit led Him into the wilderness. For 40 days and nights, Jesus went without food or water. He used this time to get close to God. Whenever He was hungry or thirsty, He went down on His knees, looked up to heaven and prayed for God's strength to come upon Him.

Jesus was so hungry and thirsty that He became weak. Satan knew this was a perfect time to tempt Jesus to make the wrong choice. He tempted Jesus with food by saying, "If You are the Son of God, tell these stones to become bread." Because Jesus was so hungry, Satan thought Jesus surely would give in. But Jesus resisted with self-control and the Word of God.

"Man does not live on bread alone," He said, "but on every word that comes from the mouth of God."

Satan was disappointed but not ready to give up yet. He tried to convince Jesus to jump off the highest point of the temple to see if His angels would catch Him. Jesus resisted with self-control and the Word of God.

"Do not put the Lord your God to the test," He told Satan.

Satan was unhappy but still not ready to give up. He told Jesus he would give Him all the kingdoms of the world if Jesus would bow down and worship him. Jesus resisted this temptation with self-control and the Word of God.

"Worship the Lord your God, and serve Him only," He said.

The Word of God was so powerful that Satan left defeated and Jesus was finally alone. Immediately, the angels of God came to assist Jesus.

Satan will try to tempt us when we are weak. He would love for us to make the wrong choices and sin.

Jesus is our example of how to resist temptation. Jesus called upon God's Word for strength to resist Satan's temptations. Jesus showed us how to have self-control and strength when we are feeling weak.

For Discussion

1. What weapon did Jesus use to avoid Satan's temptations?

2. When you are tempted, what Scripture comes to mind to help you have self-control?

Be Obedient Bracelets

Your students will make obedience bracelets to give to others in special cards.

What You Need

- resist temptation card from page 67
- permanent black markers
- white beads, 11 per child
- clear nail polish
- hole punch
- pencils
- multicolor beads, eight per child
- chenille wire
- scissors

Before Class

Duplicate the card from page 67 on colored paper for each child. Print each letter of "Be Obedient" on a different white bead using a permanent black marker. Allow time to dry, then apply polish to the beads to keep the letters from rubbing off. Make one set of beads per child. Make a sample craft to use as an example.

What to Do

1. Have the children fold the cards in half twice.
2. Instruct the children to punch two holes inside their cards where indicated.
3. Help the children fill in the left sides of their cards.
4. Show each child how to slip four multicolor beads on a chenille wire.
5. Show how to slip white beads with the word BE OBEDIENT on each chenille wire, with one blank white bead separating the words.
6. Show how to slip the four multicolor beads onto the other ends.
7. Help the children place their bracelets on their wrists to measure how much to cut off.
8. Show how to place the bracelets in the holes on the right sides of the cards and secure.

SAY Give this card to a special person. Tell your friend he or she can have self-control by wearing the Be Obedient Bracelet as a reminder to obey God's Word.

66

Do Good

Be Obedient

I THANK GOD FOR YOU

Follow God's Word

Resist Temptation

1 Corinthians 10:13

You are special because

Here is a gift that will help you to be obedient to God's Word.

Shine for Jesus

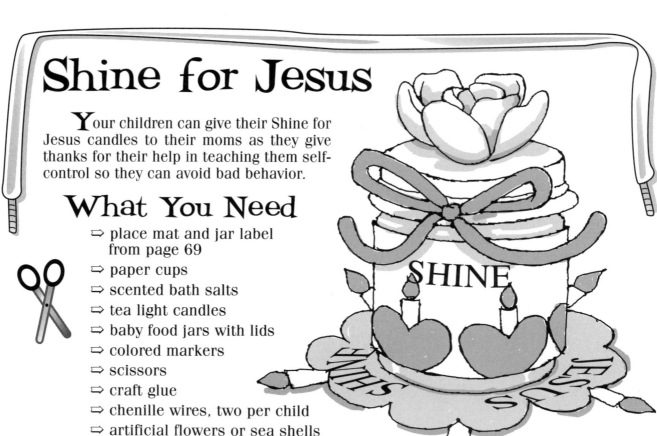

Your children can give their Shine for Jesus candles to their moms as they give thanks for their help in teaching them self-control so they can avoid bad behavior.

What You Need

- ⇨ place mat and jar label from page 69
- ⇨ paper cups
- ⇨ scented bath salts
- ⇨ tea light candles
- ⇨ baby food jars with lids
- ⇨ colored markers
- ⇨ scissors
- ⇨ craft glue
- ⇨ chenille wires, two per child
- ⇨ artificial flowers or sea shells

Before Class

Duplicate the place mat and jar label from page 69 for each child. Fill a paper cup with scented bath salts for each child. Make a sample craft to use as an example.

What to Do

1. Have each child pour half of the scented bath salts into a baby food jar.
2. Show how to place a candle on top of the bath salts and pour the remaining bath salts around the candle.
3. Instruct the children to color and cut out the place mats and jar labels.
4. Have the students close the lids on their jars.
5. Have them glue their jar labels to the outsides of their jars.
6. Show how to join two chenille wires into one and wrap them around the rim in a tied bow.
7. Have the students apply glue to the tops of their lids and press in artificial flowers or sea shells.
8. Instruct the children to apply glue to the middles of their place mats and place their jars on top.
9. Allow time to dry.

SAY

Tell your whole family how to Shine for Jesus by resisting temptation and using God's Word for self-control and strength.

SHINE   FOR   JESUS

1 Corinthians 10:13

Kindness

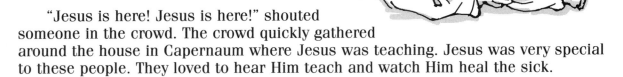

Memory Verse
*Do to others what you would have
them do to you.* ~ **Matthew 7:12**

The Kindness
of Friends
Based on Mark 2:1-12

"Jesus is here! Jesus is here!" shouted
someone in the crowd. The crowd quickly gathered
around the house in Capernaum where Jesus was teaching. Jesus was very special
to these people. They loved to hear Him teach and watch Him heal the sick.

In the city, there was a man who could not walk. Four of his friends loved him and
wanted to take him to see Jesus. They hoped that Jesus would heal their friend. So
out of the kindness of their hearts, they laid their friend on a mat. Each of the men
grabbed a corner of the mat and carried it to the front door of the house where Jesus
was teaching. But they could not enter because the crowds were too large.

So the four men carried their friend on the mat to the side of the house and
climbed the stairs to the roof. They made a large opening in the roof and, ever so
slowly, they lowered their friend down near the feet of Jesus.

Jesus was happy to see the kindness that these four men showed toward their
friend! He said to the lame man, "I tell you, get up, take your mat and go home."

The man was instantly healed! He got up, walked around and sang praises to
the Lord.

The man was thankful to have such wonderful friends and for the kindness they
showed him.

For Discussion

1. Why were these friends so kind to their lame friend?

2. What acts of kindness have you shown recently to your friends?

Stuffed with Kindness

The children will enjoy giving their friends these bags full of kindness notes to show them just how special they are.

What You Need

- ⇨ tag and notes from pages 72 and 73
- ⇨ scissors
- ⇨ hole punch
- ⇨ small lunch bags
- ⇨ chenille wires, two per child
- ⇨ craft glue
- ⇨ fabric scraps
- ⇨ shredded colored paper

Before Class

Duplicate the gift tag, words of kindness and kindness notes from pages 72 and 73 on colored paper for each child. Make a sample craft to use as an example.

What to Do

1. Have each child cut out a gift tag and punch a hole where indicated.
2. Show how to open the lunch bag and fold down the top of the bag about 3", then flatten the bag closed.
3. Instruct the students to punch two holes near the top of each bag.
4. Show how to slip a chenille wire end through one hole and secure it. Instruct the children to slip the gift tags on the chenille wires, then slip the other ends of the chenille wires through the matching holes on the same side and secure. Have them do the same with the other chenille wires for the sides without gift tags.
5. Have the students cut out and glue the words of kindness, and fabric scraps, on the outsides of their bags.
6. Show how to half-fill the insides of the bags with shredded colored paper.
7. Have the children cut out the kindness notes, or encourage them to create their own using the blank notes.
8. They should fold each note and stuff the notes inside their bags.

SAY

Think of a special friend to whom you can give your Kindness Bag. Print your friend's name, along with yours, on the gift tag. Give your bag stuffed with kindness to your special friend to see the happiness it brings. It's fun to be kind!

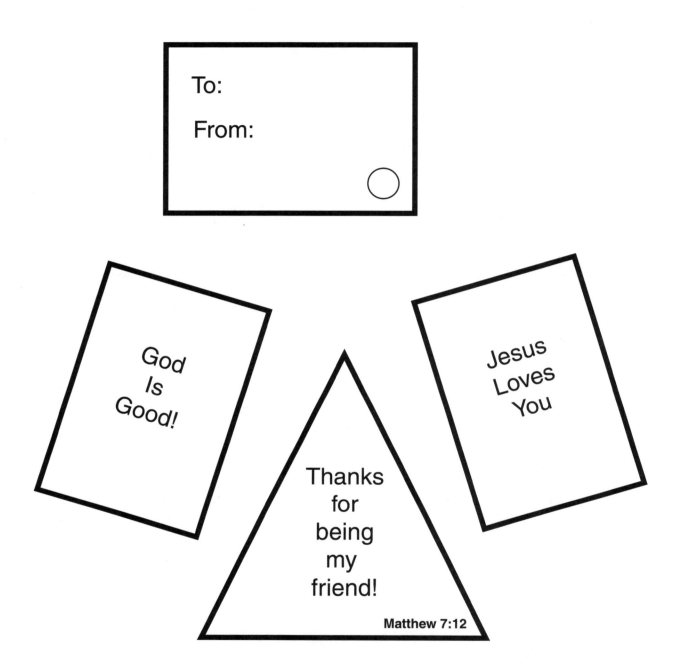

To:

From:

God
Is
Good!

Thanks
for
being
my
friend!

Matthew 7:12

Jesus
Loves
You

I will pray
for you
every day.

Ask me
about
Jesus.

I'll treat you
to an ice
cream cone!

Oh! What an Angel

Matthew 7:12

Your students can set their angels on their desks at home while they study as reminders to be kind to everyone, as angels are.

What You Need

- ⇨ angel wings from page 75
- ⇨ 1½" x 7" fabric, two per child
- ⇨ fine-tip markers
- ⇨ 2" foam balls
- ⇨ plastic forks
- ⇨ small lunch bags
- ⇨ pillow stuffing
- ⇨ chenille wires, two per child
- ⇨ craft glue
- ⇨ yarn strands or brown moss
- ⇨ 8" x 20" fabric
- ⇨ scissors
- ⇨ wooden hearts
- ⇨ 12" ribbon

Before Class

Duplicate the angel wings from page 75 on colored paper for each child. Knot one end of each 1½" x 7" fabric piece together for angel's arms. Make a sample craft to use as an example.

What to Do

1. Have each child draw eyes, mouth and cheeks on a foam ball. These will be the angels' heads. Show how to insert a plastic fork in the bottom of each head.
2. Have the students fill lunch bags with pillow stuffing for the angel bodies. Show how to insert the fork handles into the stuffing inside the bags.
3. Have the students gather the bag openings until closed and secure them with chenille wire.
4. Have the students glue yarn or moss on the tops of the heads for hair.
5. Show how to glue the 8" x 20" fabric around the bags to "dress" the angels.
6. Show how to glue the arms to the fronts of the bags and knot the ends.
7. Have the students cut out the wings and glue them to the backs of the bodies.
8. Show how to make small circles with the remaining chenille wires, cutting off the excess, and glue them to the tops of the heads for halos.
9. Have each student glue a wooden heart in the middle of an angel's praying hands.
10. Show how to tie the ribbon in a bow and glue it to the angels' hair.

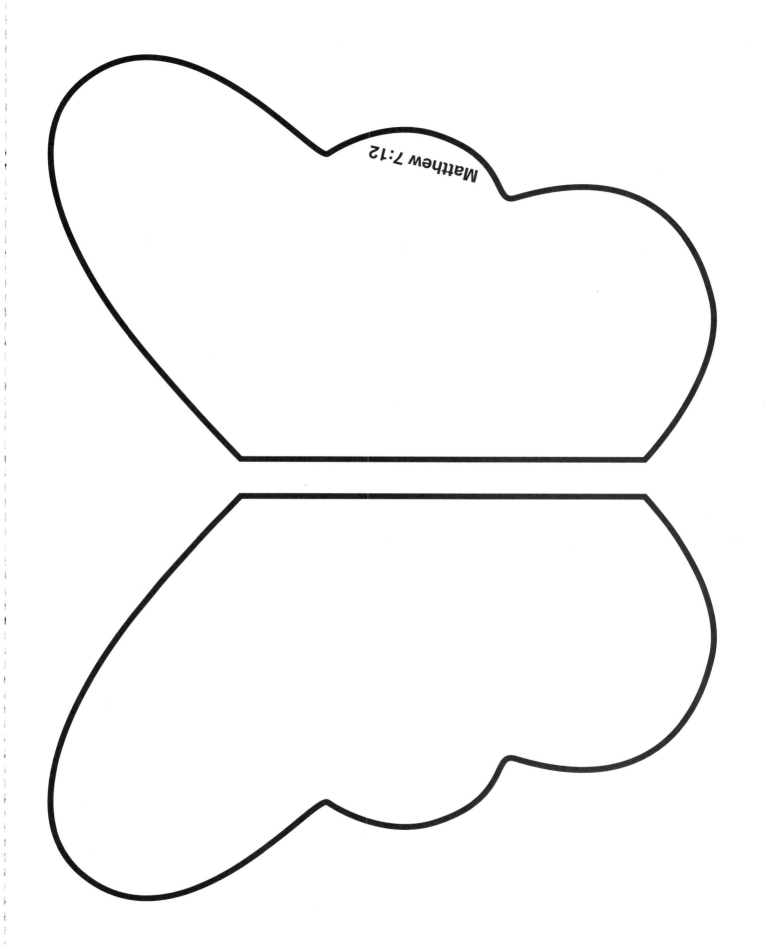

Matthew 7:12

Love
. . . .

Memory Verse

Love the Lord your God with all your heart and with all your soul and with all your mind…Love your neighbor as yourself. ~ **Matthew 22:37, 39**

Love One Another
Based on Luke 10:25-37
. . . .

One day, a lawyer asked Jesus, "What must I do to inherit eternal life?"

Jesus said if you "love your God" and "love your neighbor as yourself" you will live in heaven with Him forever.

Then the lawyer asked, "Who is my neighbor?"

Jesus loved to tell stories to help people understand His ways. He told the lawyer a story about a man who was walking along a road. He was robbed and beaten. He needed some help.

The first person who saw the injured man was a priest, but he had no love for his neighbor and immediately crossed the road to avoid him.

Then a second person, who was from the temple, came upon the injured man. Yet he, too, had no love for his neighbor. He crossed the road and ignored him.

Then a third man, a foreigner, saw the injured man. The foreigner immediately stopped to help. He cleaned up the injured man's wounds, put him on his donkey and walked along with him until they reached the city. He even paid for the injured man to stay at an inn until he was better. The third man was obedient to the Lord. Because he was from Samaria, we call him "the Good Samaritan."

The Good Samaritan not only showed unselfishness, he also showed a deep and sincere love toward his neighbor. Jesus wants us to look beyond our neighbor next door. He wants us to reach out and love the lost, especially those judged by the world to be different. When someone is in need, we as Christians should follow the example of the Good Samaritan.

For Discussion

1. When you see people who appear to be different from you, how do you treat them?

2. Tell about a time when you were a Good Samaritan, or should have been.

High in the Sky

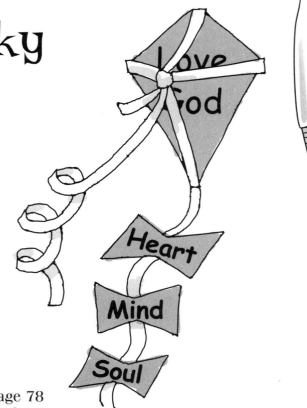

Your students will enjoy flying their kites as reminders to put God above everything else.

What You Need

⇨ kite and bows from page 78
⇨ scissors
⇨ plastic straws
⇨ black markers
⇨ craft glue
⇨ clear tape
⇨ ¼" ribbon, cut into 4", 16" and 24" lengths

Before Class

Duplicate the kite and bows from page 78 on colored paper for each child. Cut the straw lengthwise into halves (see diagram on page 78). Cut the straw halves to one 4½" and two 1½" lengths per child. Make a sample craft to use as an example.

What to Do

1. Have each child cut out a kite and bows.
2. Have the children print "love God" on the fronts of the kites and "Matthew 22:87" on the backs.
3. Show how to glue flattened 4½" straws from the top to the bottom on the backs of the kites (see diagram).
4. Instruct the students to then glue 1½" straws on either side of the longer straws and flatten them.
5. On the fronts of the kites, the students should tape the ends of 4" ribbons to the left and right corners.
6. Show how to tape one end of each 16" ribbon to the top of a kite, then how to tape the ribbons about 7" down near the bottoms of the kites, allowing the excess to hang for tails.
7. Have the children join the 4" and 16" ribbons together with 24" ribbons, allowing the excess to hang for the kites' strings.
8. Have each student print "heart" on the first bow, "soul" on the second and "mind" on the third. They should evenly space and glue the bows on the tails.

SAY

Just as a kite needs air to stay high in the sky, we need to love God with all of our hearts, souls and minds. God promises He will provide everything we need.

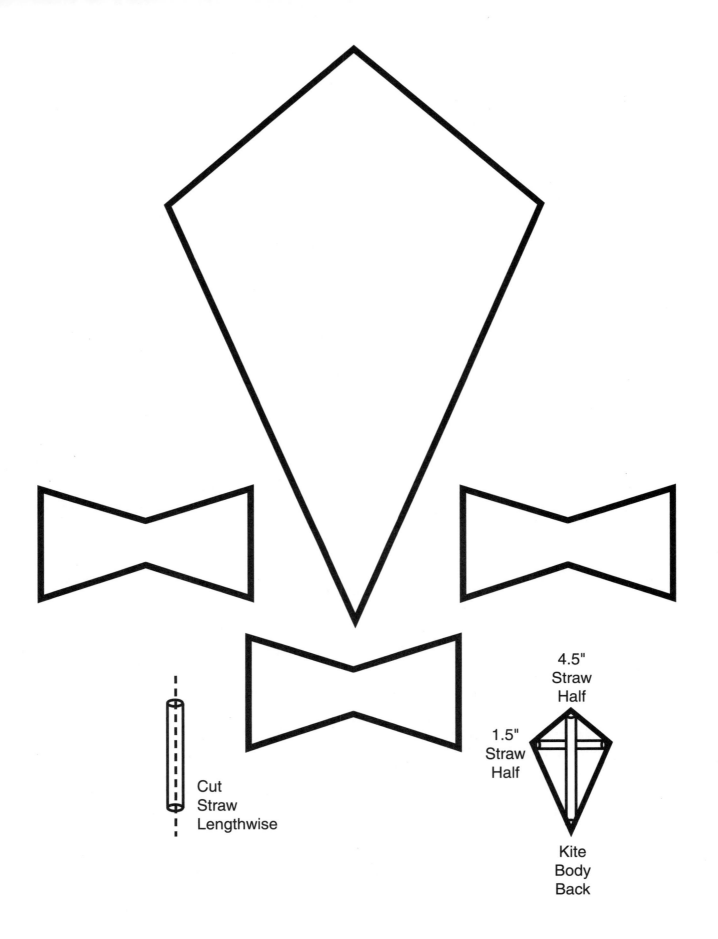

Cut
Straw
Lengthwise

4.5"
Straw
Half

1.5"
Straw
Half

Kite
Body
Back

Who Is My Neighbor?

These mini-books will remind your students to love all people, even if they appear different.

What You Need

⇨ mini-book from page 80

⇨ scissors

⇨ old magazines

⇨ hole punch

⇨ chenille wires

⇨ craft glue

⇨ shiny foil ribbon

⇨ rhinestones

⇨ colored markers

Before Class

Duplicate the mini-book from page 80 on colored paper for each child. Make a sample craft to use as an example.

What to Do

1. Have each child fold a mini-book in half twice at the dashed lines, cutting off excess paper.
2. Tell each student to punch two holes on the left side of the book where indicated.
3. Show how to pull the chenille wires through the holes and tie.
4. Instruct the students to cut open the folded edges at the bottoms of the mini-books.
5. Provide old magazines for the children to cut out pictures of people (all races, ages, cultures, etc.).
6. Have them glue the pictures in the pages of the mini-books.
7. On the fronts of the mini-books, have the students glue shiny foil ribbon strips and rhinestones.
8. Have the children write the memory verse (Matthew 22:37, 39) on the backs.
9. Allow the children to color the fronts of their mini-books.

SAY

A neighbor is not just your next-door neighbor. A neighbor is anyone! There are a variety of people in our world. God wants us to love all people, no matter how different they may appear.

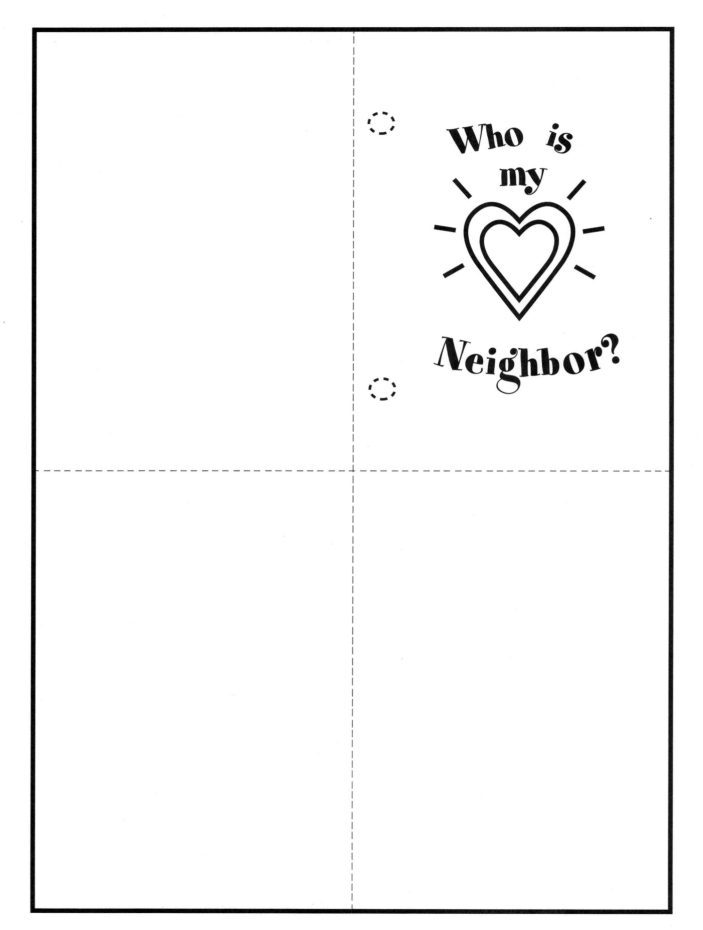

Who is
my
Neighbor?

Generosity

Memory Verse

A generous man will himself be blessed.

~ Proverbs 22:9

Special Gift for Jesus

Based on Matthew 26:1-13

With only two days left before the Passover celebration, Jesus knew that He soon would be arrested and beaten, then die on a cross for the sins of the world. The days leading up to that time were a special time, a holy time. It was a time to prepare for His upcoming burial.

While Jesus and the disciples were at the home of Simon the leper, Mary, the sister of Martha and Lazarus, arrived with a special gift for Jesus. She humbly walked over to where Jesus was sitting, held a jar above His head and slowly poured the liquid onto Him. It was a very expensive perfume.

The disciples began to discuss what Mary had just done. Some thought she was being wasteful. They thought the expensive perfume could have been sold and the money given to the poor.

When Jesus heard the disciples grumbling, He interrupted them and said, "The poor you will always have with you, but you will not always have Me."

Mary visited Jesus with a purpose. She was not concerned with the cost of the perfume. All she wanted was to give this special gift to Jesus to prepare Him for His upcoming burial. Mary's sincere generosity showed great love for Jesus.

Mary did a beautiful act. Her generous spirit was a model for all to follow in the early church, and for us today.

For Discussion

1. Why was Mary not concerned about the loss of such an expensive perfume?

2. In what ways are you generous toward God's work? How could you be more generous?

Share Your Blessings

The children will enjoy making fish to help them remember to share their blessings with others.

What You Need

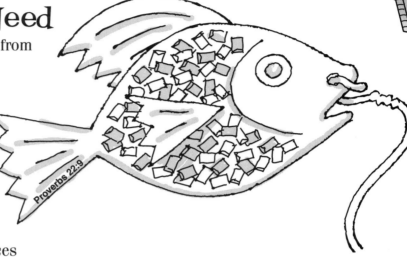

⇨ fish body and fins from page 83
⇨ paper plates, two per child
⇨ scissors
⇨ pencils
⇨ hole punch
⇨ colored markers
⇨ craft glue
⇨ chenille wires, two per child
⇨ colored straw pieces

Before Class

Duplicate the fish body and fins from page 83 on heavy paper for each child and cut out the individual items. Make a sample craft to use as an example.

What to Do

1. Have each child align the back fin on the fish body with the paper plate's ruffled edge, trace the fish onto the plate and cut it out.

2. Instruct the students to draw the eyes of the fish as shown on the pattern.

3. Show where to punch holes near the fish's mouths where indicated.

4. Show how to align Fin A with the ruffled edges of another paper plate and cut it out. Do the same for Fin B.

5. Allow the students to color Fins A and B and the back fins on the paper plate fish bodies.

6. Show how to glue Fin A to the front of the fish and Fin B to the back of the fish.

7. Instruct each student to combine two chenille wires into one and curl one end to resemble the hook on a fishing line.

8. Help the students apply plenty of glue to the fish bodies and drop straw pieces on the glue until the bodies are completely covered. Allow to dry.

SAY

Jesus fed 5,000 people with what started out as five loaves and two fish. Jesus performed a miracle! God promises to always provide for our needs, but He likes for us to help Him provide for others. When you know people who are hungry or in need, see if you can find ways in which your family can share your blessings with them. Jesus wants us to be generous.

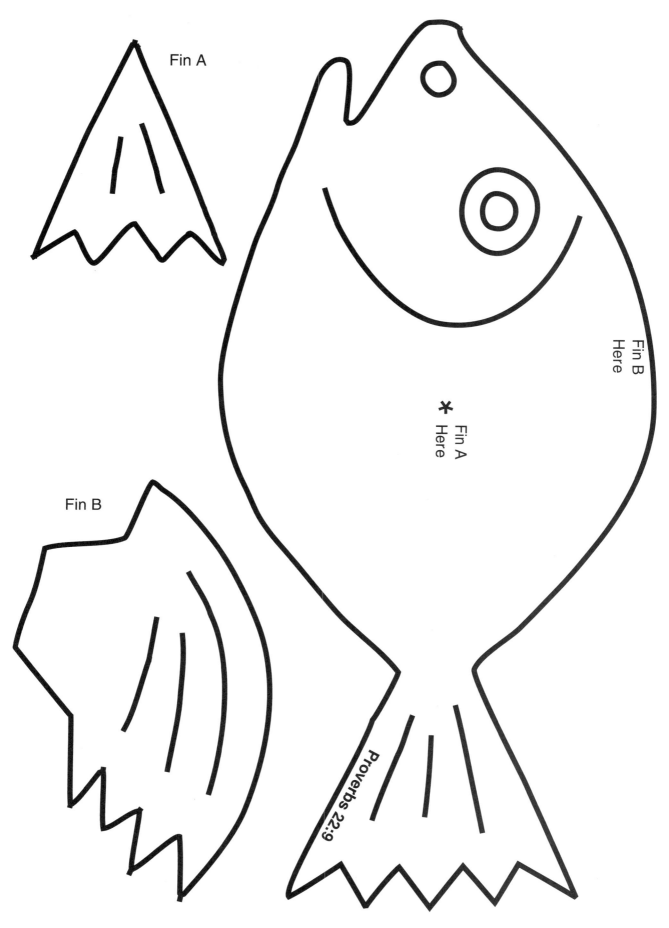

Fin A

Fin B
Here

Fin A
Here

Fin B

Proverbs 22:9

83

Making Time Milk Shake

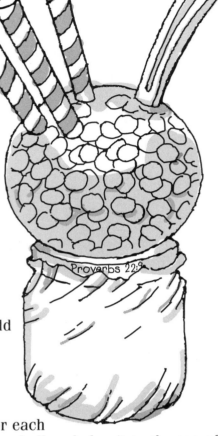

After this craft, whenever the children enjoy a chocolate milk shake, it will be a reminder to them to make time for others.

What You Need

⇨ giving slips on page 85
⇨ 3" foam balls
⇨ craft glue
⇨ baby food jars with lids
⇨ brown construction paper
⇨ hole punch
⇨ aluminum foil
⇨ scissors
⇨ colored plastic straws, three per child
⇨ plastic spoon handles
⇨ paper plates

Before Class

Duplicate the giving slips on page 85 for each child. Slice off a large portion of the foam ball and glue it to the top of the baby food jar lid. Allow time to dry. Make confetti from brown construction paper using a hole punch. Make a sample craft to use as an example.

What to Do

1. Have the children cover the outsides of the baby food jars with foil.
2. Instruct each child to choose three of the six giving slips, cut them out and place them inside a jar.
3. Have the students place the lids on the jars and write "Proverbs 22:9" on the rims of the lids.
4. Show how to stick three different colors of straw ends into the foam balls, cutting off the excess.
5. Show how to stick the plastic spoon handles into the foam balls.
6. Have the students place paper plates underneath their jars.
7. Instruct the students to apply plenty of craft glue to the foam ball.
8. Show how to sprinkle brown confetti on the glue until the foam is covered. Allow time to dry.

SAY Who loves chocolate milk shakes? Every time you enjoy a chocolate milk shake, take out one of your giving slips from your jar. Make a promise to give your time to do whatever it says. Do it for the Lord!

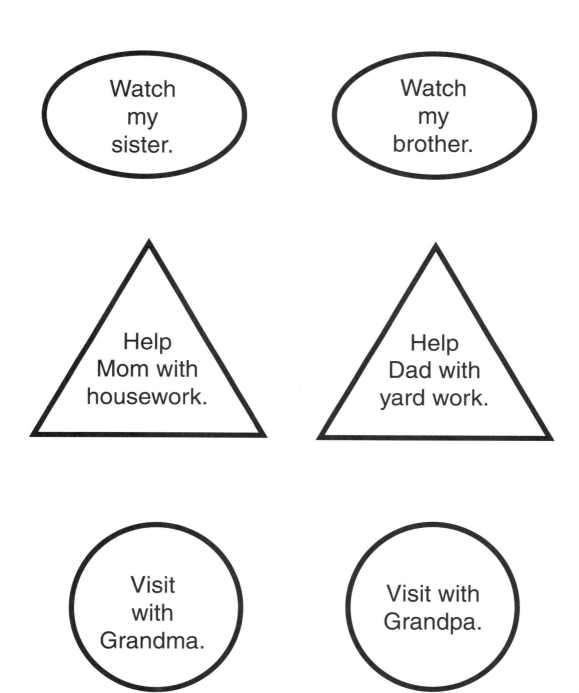

Watch my sister.

Watch my brother.

Help Mom with housework.

Help Dad with yard work.

Visit with Grandma.

Visit with Grandpa.

Unselfishness

Memory Verse

If anyone would come after me, he must deny himself and take up his cross daily and follow me. ~ **Luke 9:23**

Jesus, Our Best Example
Based on Genesis 3; Mark 8:31-34

After Adam and Eve selfishly ate the forbidden apple and disobeyed God, their sin separated generations and generations of people from God.

Then God, unselfishly through His grace, came down to earth as a man named Jesus. He gave us an opportunity to take away the sin that separates us from Him. Jesus was rejected, suffered and died on a cross so we could humble ourselves and accept Him into our hearts and lives.

While Jesus was on earth, He also taught the disciples that they needed to treat others as more important than themselves. Jesus showed them through miracles and kind acts how to respond unselfishly to different situations.

There were many times when Jesus had to correct His disciples. Once, Jesus was telling a crowd of people, "The Son of Man must suffer many things and be rejected by the elders, chief priests and teachers of the law, and then He must be killed and after three days rise again."

Peter didn't want these things to happen to Jesus, so he told Jesus He was wrong. Jesus turned to Peter and the disciples and said, "You do not have in mind the things of God, but the things of men." Jesus was trying to teach Peter and the disciples, as well as the crowd, that people's ways are selfish, but God's ways are unselfish.

To learn to be unselfish, you must learn to put others before you. Jesus wants His people to serve others rather than be served. Most importantly, He want us to tell everyone about Him.

For Discussion

1. What was Jesus trying to teach?

2. What kinds of things do you do to put others before you?

Grow Up in Christ Chart

Help your students learn to be less selfish and more like Jesus by practicing these truths.

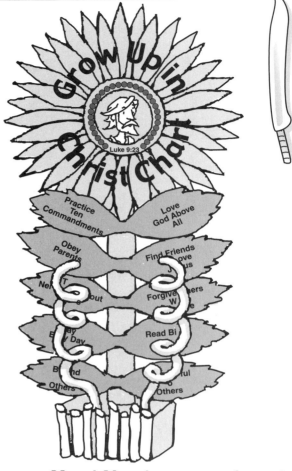

What You Need

⇨ sunflower and leaves from pages 88 and 89
⇨ craft foam squares
⇨ small boxes or lids
⇨ scissors
⇨ 2" colored straws, five per child
⇨ 3" colored straws, five per child
⇨ wooden rulers
⇨ yellow, brown and green markers
⇨ craft glue
⇨ chenille wires, two per child

Before Class

Duplicate the sunflower and leaves from pages 88 and 89 on heavy paper for each child. Fit a craft foam square inside each child's box lid. Cut one end of each straw into a V-shape. Insert one ruler into each craft foam square with the blank side facing forward, one per child. Make a sample craft to use as an example.

What to Do

1. Have the children color the petals on the sunflowers yellow, the small circles around the pictures of Jesus brown and the leaves green.
2. Instruct the students to cut out the sunflowers and leaves.
3. Have them glue the sunflowers to the tops of their rulers.
4. Have the students glue the leaves, evenly-spaced, down the rest of the rulers.
5. Show how to curl the chenille wires and insert them into the craft foam, one on each side of the sunflower.
6. Have the students glue down straws with the V shapes on top, alternating sizes on the fronts of the boxes (for fences).

SAY On each leaf is a different truth or character quality of Jesus. Pick one leaf at the bottom of the sunflower to practice throughout the week. The next week, I will remind you to practice the next truth. We will continue each week until you reach the top of your sunflower. After practicing the last truth, we will have a celebration to share how each of us has grown up in Christ.

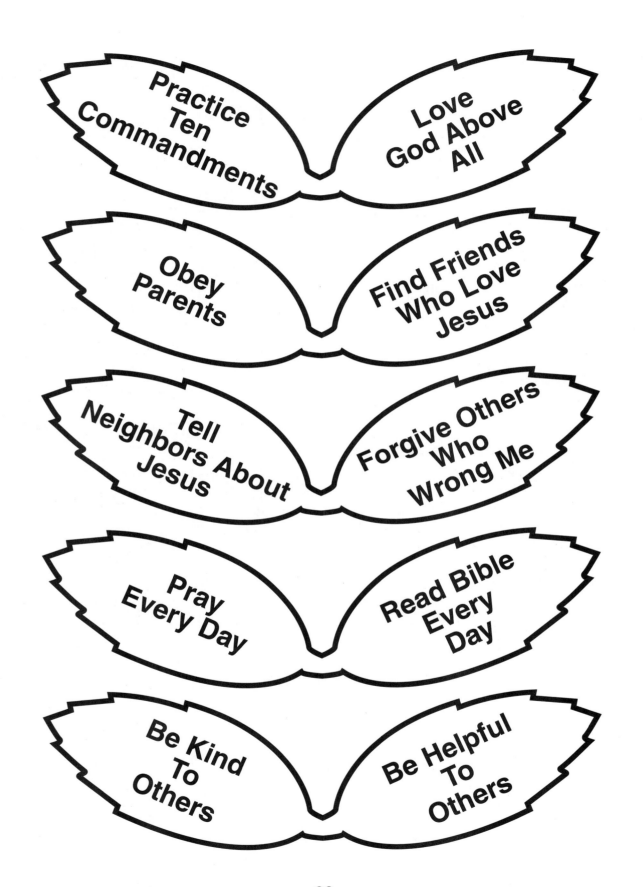

Practice Ten Commandments

Love God Above All

Obey Parents

Find Friends Who Love Jesus

Tell Neighbors About Jesus

Forgive Others Who Wrong Me

Pray Every Day

Read Bible Every Day

Be Kind To Others

Be Helpful To Others

Grow Up In Christ Chart

Luke 9:23

Friends Care

Help the students learn to offer their time to help others, as Jesus did.

What You Need

⇨ gift certificate from page 91

⇨ scissors

⇨ pencils

⇨ legal-size envelopes

⇨ chenille wire

⇨ craft glue

Before Class

Duplicate the gift certificate from page 91 on colored paper for each child. Make a sample craft to use as an example.

What to Do

1. Have the children cut out the gift certificates.

2. Suggest that they think of special people to give their gift certificates. Give the children suggestions as to what the gifts could be (for example: "I will help you with your math homework"). Some children may want to think of their own ideas.

3. Have the students fill in the blanks on the gift certificates.

4. Have them fold the gift certificates in half, insert them in the envelopes and seal the envelopes.

5. Show how to form the letters FRIENDS CARE using the chenille wire and cutting off any excess. Have the students glue the letters to the fronts of their envelopes. Allow time to dry.

SAY You can be unselfish like Jesus by offering your time to help others. Give your envelope to someone, and be sure to do what the gift certificate says!

Gift Certificate

To:

From:

I will:

Luke 9:23

Salvation

Memory Verse
Believe in the Lord Jesus, and you will be saved – you and your household. ~ Acts 16:31

A Shaken Jailer Believes

Based on Acts 16:16-34

Paul and Silas were traveling from city to city to tell others about Jesus. Many people accepted Jesus and asked to be baptized. Some business owners, who made money from people visiting the city to see fortune tellers, were not happy about this. So they decided to drag Paul and Silas to the authorities. Paul and Silas were beaten and thrown into jail.

But being in jail did not stop Paul and Silas. They continued singing and praying about Jesus even though they were locked up.

Outside the door was a jailer whose job was to keep watch over all prisoners. He heard Paul and Silas praising Jesus. He was curious about this Messiah. He also was keeping a watchful eye on Paul and Silas so they would not escape; otherwise, he would be killed for not doing his job.

One night while the jailer took a nap, there was an earthquake. When the ground shook, the jail doors opened and the prisoners were released from their chains. They were free to escape!

The jailer was shaken up by the earthquake. When he realized what had happened, he feared that the prisoners had escaped. The jailer was ready to take his life because he knew the authorities would not understand how they had escaped.

But Paul shouted to him, "Don't harm yourself! We are all here!" The jailer was in shock but very thankful. The jailer then knew Paul and Silas were in the jail so he could learn more about Jesus.

The jailer asked them, "Sirs, what must I do to be saved?"

They replied, "Believe in the Lord Jesus and you will be saved."

The jailer accepted Jesus and promised to live for Him. The jailer was so excited about his commitment to the Lord, he brought home Paul and Silas to meet his family. His family could see how much the jailer had changed, so they all accepted Jesus, too, and were baptized.

For Discussion

1. What about Jesus are you curious to know?

2. Do you know people who need to accept Jesus? What will you say to them?

Ask Jesus into Your Heart

Encourage the children to place their magnets where their friends will ask: "What does John 3:16 mean?"

What You Need

⇨ heart from page 94
⇨ scissors
⇨ 4" craft sticks, two per child
⇨ 2" foam balls ⇨ 2" red ribbons
⇨ colored markers ⇨ 2" gold chenille wires
⇨ craft glue ⇨ magnets

Before Class

Duplicate the heart from page 94 on heavy paper for each child. Cut a craft stick in half and glue half to the top of another craft stick to form a cross, one per child. Slice the foam balls in half so you have one half per child. Print on the chalkboard: "For God so loved the world that He gave his one and only Son, that whoever believes in Him shall not perish but have eternal life. John 3:16." Make a sample craft to use as an example.

What to Do

1. Have each child color and cut out a heart. The children should write GOD across the tops of their hearts.
2. Instruct the students to color the foam ball halves to look like earth (blue for water, brown for earth).
3. Show where to glue the crosses to the middles of the hearts.
4. Show how to fold the red ribbons in half and glue where the crosses intersect.
5. Show how to form circles with gold chenille wire for a "crown of thorns" and glue on top of the ribbons.
6. Have the students glue the "worlds" at the bottoms of the crosses. Using black markers, they should print "John" on the left and "3:16" on the right of the "worlds."
7. Give each student a magnet to glue to the back of his or her heart.

SAY

Here is an easy way to memorize John 3:16! I will slowly read John 3:16 from the board and point to my craft. Do what I do. Point to "God" on your craft and say, "For God." Outline the edges of your heart with your finger and say, "So loved." Point to the world and say, "The world." Point to "God" and the crown of thorns and say, "That He gave His one and only Son." Point to each other and say, "That whoever believes in Him." Point to heaven and say, "Shall not perish but have eternal life."

93

Forgive as the Lord Forgave You

The students can hang these double plaques on their walls to remind them that forgiveness is an important step to salvation.

FORGIVE
AS THE LORD

FORGAVE
YOU.
Colossians 3:13

What You Need

- ⇨ squares from page 96
- ⇨ scissors
- ⇨ clear, six-pocket photo pages
- ⇨ hole punch
- ⇨ chenille wires, two per child
- ⇨ craft glue
- ⇨ craft sticks, eight per child
- ⇨ colored markers

Before Class

Duplicate the squares from page 96 on colored paper for each child. Cut two pockets from the clear photo pages for each child. Make a sample craft to use as an example.

What to Do

1. Have the children cut out the squares.
2. Show how to insert a square into each clear photo pocket.
3. Instruct each student to punch a hole on each corner of the top photo pocket and to punch holes on the top (left and right) of the bottom photo pocket.
4. Show how to slip one end of a chenille wire into the top left and the other end into the top right of the top photo pocket, securing the chenille wire ends.
5. Have the students cut the remaining chenille wires in half.
6. Show how to attach the photo pockets together by slipping one end of a chenille wire into the bottom left hole of the first photo pocket and the other end into the top left hole of the second photo pocket, securing the ends. Then do the same for the other side.
7. Have the students glue four craft sticks around each photo pocket border.
8. Allow the children to color the craft sticks.

SAY

Jesus is our ultimate example of how to forgive others. When you are hurt, God gives you the wonderful opportunity to act like Him. We can give a blessing to those who wrong us by forgiving them. Our actions may draw them to salvation in Jesus, too.

FORGIVE AS THE LORD

FORGAVE YOU.
Colossians 3:13